ORFF
Day by Day

Classroom projects in
music and movement

ALICE BRASS

Illustrations by
NAZY SAKHAVARZ

ROBIN BRASS STUDIO
Toronto

Robin Brass Studio Inc.
www.rbstudiobooks.com

Printed and bound in Canada by Marquis Imprimeur,
Cap-Saint-Ignace, Quebec

ISBN-13: 978-1-896941-02-8
ISBN-10: 1-896941-02-8

Cover Design: Molly Brass
Illustrations: Nazy Sakhavarz

National Library of Canada Cataloguing in Publication

Brass, Alice, 1941–

Orff day by day : classroom projects in music and movement /
Alice Brass; illustrations by Nazy Sakhavarz.

ISBN 1-896941-02-8

1. School music – Instruction and study – Activity programs. 2. Music
– Instruction and study – Juvenile. 3. Xylophone music – Teaching
pieces. I. Sakhavarz, Nazy, 1972– . II. Title. III. Title: Classroom projects in music and movement.

MT10.B823 1997   372.87'044   C2003-900966-1

Contents

ACKNOWLEDGEMENTS

I would like to thank the children and the parents of the children at Courcelette Public School in Scarborough and Claude Watson School for the Arts in North York (both public elementary schools in Toronto) for their inspiration and their enthusiasm which have encouraged me to write this material.

Thanks also to Joan Sumberland, who encouraged me, as a volunteer parent, to try some Orff with the children. I started with children in grade 8, not the normal place for Orff, but they truly enjoyed it and I was encouraged to do more.

Lois Birkenshaw-Fleming, author of many of our Canadian books on music for young children, has been a great support through my years at Claude Watson. She taught me to be free and creative with Orff and to allow and encourage the children to lead the way. For this I owe her much gratitude. She also read through a rough draft of this book and her many suggestions were very helpful.

Thanks also to Dale Hyde, Laurence Gilman, and Carole Smiley, who read the manuscript and offered very helpful suggestions. Thank you to my family, who listen to endless tales of the wonderful children I teach and have always encouraged me to continue.

The Introduction is adapted from an article written in collaboration with my daughter, Zoë Brass, for *The Recorder*, the publication of the Ontario Music Educators' Association. It explains why I think an Orff class is such an important addition to any elementary classroom.

Nazy Sakhavarz, who created the illustrations, has brought the book to life. I have known Nazy since she was a young student at Claude Watson School for the Arts and have always admired her work.

Alice Brass

Orff Planning Outlines

My objective is to give teachers a plan of how to proceed through an Orff project using all the various Orff concepts of music, drama, language, movement, and rhythm. I have concentrated on the form and structure of the music, assuming that other parts of the music program – good vocal technique, note reading to name only two – will be taught concurrently.

It is not necessary to complete every step and teachers should read each set carefully using only what works for them. All classes will react differently and as a teacher you have to be prepared to change your plans on the fly.

WHAT IS ORFF OR THE ORFF APPROACH?

The Orff approach allows the children to explore how music is created and what role they can have in its creation. It encourages them to react to music, not only the notes but the form and the rhythm. This reaction is in turn expressed by clapping, body percussion, chants, singing and/or playing instruments that Carl Orff designed in such a way that they are very simple to learn to use. A certain amount of technical ability is essential as in any art discipline before it is possible to be creative.

It is very important that children learn to sing, read notes and perhaps play a conventional instrument. The Orff approach is not intended to replace these skills but to enhance them. If you have only a short period of time each week to teach music, then you will have to combine Orff and regular music teaching. These lesson plans could be combined with note reading, solfege, good singing tone, etc. However, I have concentrated on the creative side of the projects.

It has also been my experience that an accomplished orchestral player can happily share an Orff class with children who cannot yet read music. Neither one of these extremes is either bored or frustrated and only sees the joy of music and of participation.

If you are new to the Orff approach, I encourage you to try it and attend Orff workshops and courses to give you more material and ideas of how to use the children's ingenuity to make music fun for all.

THE CREATIVE PROCESS

When you are asking children to be creative and work in groups on such projects, you must be prepared for some noise and apparent disorganization.

Note: I try to limit this open creativity to ten minute stretches but you must let the children *play* a bit if you are to see the magic a child can bring to a situation.

The younger the class the shorter the time they can focus on such open-ended ideas as "What would you do with this?" I have them perform for each other long before their ideas are complete to keep returning them to their tasks.

You will find that three or four children to a group is plenty. More than that and arguments get in the way of creativity. Once the ideas are firm the groups can often be amalgamated to create a more interesting production.

I have **some parameters** which I enforce because they work for me

1. "No sex or violence in Orff." By this I mean no mock fights, no bad language, and no bathroom jokes. The children sometimes argue and say that this is unrealistic but I am very firm and tell them not in Orff. Such ideas might be saved for older classes in drama.

2. Another area in which I am very firm is that each group must be able to perform something, usually at the end of each class. A lack of performance is not acceptable. There are excellent performances and good performances, and perhaps silly performances but **the only unacceptable performances are the ones that don't happen.**

A WORD ABOUT THE MUSIC

With each piece of music I have suggested what I think is essential and other elements that may be of interest. You should feel free to **use whichever parts of this music work for your class.** The instrumentation is my suggestion but is certainly not the only way to do it. For instance I do not like using B flats and F sharps – because this often leads to mis-placing the natural Fs and Bs. So wherever possible I change these notes in the accompaniment to some other note that will work. If this housekeeping problem is easy for you to manage, then these notes can be used very effectively.

THE ORDER OF THE PROJECTS

The projects are not in any particular order except for the ones on improvisation. These sections on improvisation should be tackled in order even if not in their entirety. The remaining sections can be tackled in any order that works with the rest of your program. Please feel free to change any of the material to suit your purposes. I have provided pages at the beginning of each project for your own notes.

Orff
Music and Movement and Fun

It may sound quite unbelievable that accomplished concert musicians can happily coexist with beginner musicians in any kind of "music class". This happens every day, however, during Orff classes at the Claude Watson School for the Arts. Here students take part in a program of half-day academics and half-day arts. The arts curriculum is diverse, spanning dance, drama, music, and visual arts. For the grade 4 and grade 5 students, the music program includes three half-hour periods per week of Orff. These classes are not meant to teach the children singing techniques, specific instruments, or to read music. They are meant to allow the children to explore how music is created and what role they can have in its creation.

When he developed his ideas, Carl Orff intended to help dancers better relate their movement to the music to which they were dancing. He observed that ballet dancers were only conscious of the beats of the music and consequently their dancing did not reflect musical phrasing. With so much time spent in the dance studio, these dancers had never had the time to learn an instrument which would give them insight into the making of the music. With this realization, Carl Orff designed instruments that would be simple to learn to play, so that the dancers could explore the creation of music and understand how it made them feel.

MUSIC FOR CHILDREN

Carl Orff's techniques were quickly recognized for their application in teaching music and movement to school children, who could learn to feel and move to the music they were making. The students were not required to learn complex techniques about sound production or dancing steps. Instead, they were encouraged to explore the way sounds could be combined with movement to create a united package. One of the focuses of Orff is on music as a combination of sounds rather than notes. Once children

learn to put sounds together in a pleasing manner, they can appreciate how the pitches and timbres of different instruments can be put together to form a piece of music. By further combining these sounds with the thoughts they evoke, movement evolves naturally. Alternatively, movement can be used to evoke sounds or music. Students can learn to use physical levels, spaces, and modes of movement if they are asked to interpret the sounds they hear. When they themselves are creating the sounds, a personal connection is made to the music and physical interpretation is that much more genuine.

An important aspect of music is the feeling of rhythm; this is one area that often gets neglected as children struggle to learn how to read notes on a page, or fingerings on an instrument. Orff emphasizes rhythm and the role it plays in the structure of music. From their first Orff class, students can create simple rhythm patterns by using their hands. Solo, or in a group, clapping is one of the simplest ways to explore the patterns of rhythm. Some students' creations may be more dynamic than others, but each child can have the experience of creating a little bit of music without years of formal training.

ORFF CAN SPOT ACADEMIC PROBLEM AREAS

The benefits of Orff as a teaching tool go far beyond the musical realm. Working with children in an Orff class can give a great deal of insight into their activities during the rest of the day. It is often difficult to pinpoint exactly why a child is having difficulty learning and responding to teaching as we think he or she should. The inability to understand patterns and difficulty using those patterns in problem-solving both in mathematics and language provide a roadblock to learning for many children. One of the useful side effects of Orff is its value in identifying these sequencing and co-ordination problems. Often these problem areas may go undetected in the classroom setting.

ORFF – AN ENHANCMENT TO A MUSIC PROGRAM

Although Orff has many useful applications, it is not always a substitute for other types of music programs, either instrumental or vocal. These types of classes teach totally separate things, and are equally as important in the development of the child. Students often need to learn the discipline and technique that comes with a formal music program. Few students will find a position for themselves in a professional symphony with only their Orff skills. They may, however, have learned to enjoy music during their Orff classes, and this could lead to further musical pursuits. An Orff program enhances the more disciplined music program, by giving children the chance to make those explorations for which there might not be time in a choir or band rehearsal.

INTEGRATION OF THE ARTS AND ACADEMICS

The valuable process of integrating the various arts areas as well as bringing together arts and academics can be handled naturally through an Orff program. Since exploration of music is an important part of Orff, children can create music to go with poetry and stories from language arts and drama, or with patterns and shapes in mathematics. Since Orff is used around the world, music from other geographical areas can be used, thereby stimulating interest in geography and history. I have discovered that children love to interpret art with their own movement, to which they can add music they have created or music that is already part of the literature. The most exciting aspect of this type of integration is that it is often developed by the children themselves when they think they are playing and don't notice they are working.

THE TEACHER MUST BE A MUSICIAN WHO IS INTERESTED IN MOVEMENT

While Orff is aimed at both musicians and non-musicians, the teacher must have a solid understanding of the structure of music. The teacher should be able to explain why the music created by the students sounds the way it does and as well must be able to evaluate which aspects of music will be valuable to the Orff learning process. It may be necessary to compile small bits of material from songs, poetry, written music, or student-created work. The apparent simplicity of Orff is for the children only. It is not a technique to be used by the untrained musician.

Teachers using the Orff approach will benefit greatly from a background in movement. Knowledge of all the ways a body can move is essential. As well, an understanding of movement through time, space and the child's available energy is essential to guide students through this learning process. The children will do the moving but the teacher must be able to discuss their ideas, suggest alternatives and stretch their imaginations.

SUITABLE AGE GROUPS TO ENJOY ORFF

Although Orff can be beneficial in almost any stage of a person's education, an ideal time to begin is around the age of eight. At this time, children are still relatively uninhibited about being creative in front of their peers, and yet they have developed the skills necessary to take full advantage of Orff techniques. Many early childhood programs use Orff methods at ages younger than this. Certainly Orff can add much to this kind of program, but unfortunately many children leave Orff behind just at the age when it would be most useful. It is also false to assume that if children have not been exposed to Orff by the time they are ten years old, that they will not be able to benefit from the experience. The Orff program at Claude Watson extends officially only into grade 6. However, many students in grade 7 and 8 come to see if they can *help* the younger children develop their ideas. As well, some students from the high school come back to the public school to help out with the Orff performances.

One group of grade 8 students in a regular academic school, most of whom were non-musicians with no previous music training, successfully put on a performance of an Orff type arrangement of pop music using recorders, xylophones, and various noise makers.

ORFF IS FUN

With all the technical advantages of Orff set aside, it is fun for the children and it shows no prejudice. Possessing great violin playing skills does not mean that combining a poem with sounds and movement will be boring. Likewise, the complete beginner at music will have just as much valuable input into a project as all the other students. As one student exclaimed when asked what people should be told about Orff, "Tell them it's instruments, tell them it's moving, and tell them it's fun!"

Orff is not about literal interpretation of music, or telling the children how it should be done. Orff is about how music makes the children feel and their insight into why it makes them feel that way.

Fall in the Forests

In this unit the students learn to express their feelings about autumn. They identify certain aspects of nature that affect the way we think and feel, such as colour and sound.

They learn through the art the way others have expressed their feelings in colours about this period of the year.

Poetry, particularly verse such as Haiku, gives the children a way to express their own feelings about nature.

They will learn a Canadian folk song and work on the technical co-ordination necessary for creating an accompaniment.

They are continuing to work on their group skills to produce an excellent presentation.

Notes and Inspiration

Fall in the Forests

DAY 1 – THOUGHTS ABOUT FALL

Discuss what happens to the forests in fall: the leaves, animals, storms and so on.

Encourage some brief dreamy thoughts about fall in the forests. The following Haiku-type poem makes an excellent example:

A single red leaf darting as it falls
reminds us of summer fun.

You could read some other Haiku poetry or find other poems that are short and simple.

If you think it will help, give the children an outline with which to start.

For example:
Yellow is _____
Red and orange _____

or

A babbling brook _____
A bear cub _____
The rain pelted down and _____

The children can give their ideas orally or they can work in groups and write them down. Encourage the children to stretch their ideas once they begin to come up with anything at all.

Some examples:

The child might say, "Yellow leaves make the trees glow in the sunshine."

This could be stretched to "Yellow leaves make the trees glow in the sunshine and it reminds me of a hot summer day."

or "Yellow makes the leaves look dressed for a big celebration".

The child might say, "The rain pelted down and ruined the flowers."

This could be stretched to "The rain pelted down and ruined the flowers that I had planned to give to my friend for her birthday."

or "The rain pelted down making such a load noise on the roof that I could not hear the television and it was my favourite show."

Their creations can of course be developed in any direction you want depending on your classroom needs. When you find a really good idea amongst the children's work, I recommend reading it to the class so they understand better what you want. Even though my classes are only thirty minutes I always show group work for the last part of the class. It encourages the whole class to expand their ideas.

DAY 2 — PICTURES OF FALL

Show the class some pictures of fall by some artists. I would choose the Group of Seven plus Tom Thomson but you may of course choose differently. If you have art classes with the children you could use their pictures from a fall project as well.

Talk a bit about the paintings, the subject matter, the artists, and how and why the pictures were painted.

Perhaps the children would like to dramatize their impressions of the paintings. They can do this spontaneously or you can give them some time in small groups to work out their ideas. This will depend on how well the children work together. If you decide to let them play with the ideas in small groups, I suggest you allow only about 8 to 10 minutes before asking for some performances. The ideas will not yet be complete but this allows those having difficulty to see the ideas of others and also serves to keep the children focused. Too much time allows for lack of focus, restlessness and subsequent control problems.

You must realize that after such a short period of time the ideas will not be finished but these mini performances will encourage all the groups to try something. Be sure to let the children know that you are not expecting a finished product.

DAY 3 — DRAMAS ABOUT THE THOUGHTS

Continue the activities of day 1 and day 2. Combine some of the Haiku or poetry ideas with the dramas about the paintings. Be sure to have performance opportunities at every session so the class can see the work in progress.

DAY 4 — SOUND EFFECTS TO ADD TO THE DRAMAS

The children love to add sound effects to their creations. The noise level can be a problem once they add sounds so I control this by allowing *only one* percussion instrument per group to enhance the performance. This is usually plenty for them to concentrate on along with their creations.

If the development of their poems into dramas takes 3 or 4 days instead of 1 or 2, do not be alarmed. Being creative often takes a lot more time than following preset instructions.

DAY 5 – TEACH THE SONG

Teach the melody and words to *Land of the Silver Birch*.

Many of the children may already know the words.

Probably on the first day you will be able to add the drumming rhythm. The suggested rhythm would be played throughout. Talk about the piece and ask the children for other suitable drum rhythms that could go with this piece. Ask for suggestions of other percussion instruments on which to play this rhythm. By the end of this class the melody for this piece should be well known.

DAY 6 — LEARN THE OSTINATO PARTS

The children should be ready to learn the Orff instrumental parts.

Start with the xylophone part – DABA. If the children are experienced players, this will be easy. If they are beginners, remove the C's, E's, F's and G's to make it easier to see the notes. This is a good exercise because their left hand must cross over the right to play the B. You can talk about good mallet technique. This exercise will show you very quickly any child who cannot cross the midline.

(Note to teachers: Often a child who has problems with note sequences will experience difficulty with math and other sequential learning problems. Noting this will help you to help them in other areas.)

The class can then sing the song with this accompaniment and add the various percussion rhythms they developed previously. If none of these rhythms work well, you can give them the one that is here or one of your own.

You can probably also add the bass part today.

Hint: Always put one of the strongest musicians on the bass. The part is easy but if it is not solid the whole piece falls apart.

DAY 7 — DISCUSS THE INSTRUMENTATION

Review the music for *Land of the Silver Birch*. Add any other instrumental parts you want, glockenspiel for decoration, metallophone to help the bass, soprano xylophone for added rhythmic interest. None of these are necessary but you can experiment to see what you and your students like. I have given you some suggestions but choose only what works for you and your group.

It is important that you discuss the effects of the various instruments on the parts that they are playing. This will help the children to learn to listen and to be critical of the music they play and hear.

One effective approach is to switch the instruments around on the various parts and then decide which arrangement seems to work best. You will find there is not always agreement on this. We all hear sound differently.

DAY 8 – PUT THE MUSIC WITH THE DRAMAS

Put the music together with the drama and the poetry. You might want to try a Rondo: i.e., song, drama, song, poem, song, drama and poem together, song. You will have to decide if you want to choose certain dramas or have one from every group in the class.

Another idea is to introduce the dramas with the song, then present the dramas altogether and end with a bit of, or all of, the song.

Yet another idea is to have the students place themselves in the painting and sing about the pictures while acting them out.

Day 8 could be extended to days 8, 9, 10. After that you may want to do a performance for an assembly or for another class.

Alternatively, day 8 could be the end of this project and you could move on to a something new.

Question and Answer
A Rondo

Form in the arts, as in other academic disciplines, is very important. The structure of a piece of music or creative presentation helps the creator to express the feelings of the piece. Balance is always important whether the creation is music, art, dance or drama.

The two forms discussed in this set of classes are (1) question and answer, the form on which much music is based, and (2) Rondo, a longer form where many questions and answers are joined together to make one long composition. The example of a rondo which is often used is that of a many-layered sandwich where the bread is the A section while the various fillings are the B, C, D etc. sections. The rondo is then put together as follows: ABACADA. Each section is often, though not always, a complete question and answer.

This set of lessons explores the various extensions of question and answer using only rhythmic instruments or found sounds, that is sounds found around the class – rattling paper, keys on desks, pencil sharpener squeaking. In this set of lessons, the technical problems of playing a melodic instrument do not become a factor.

The rondo form is used to co-ordinate all the various questions and answers created. To make the rondo effective requires exploration of sound and the discussion of the contrasting nature of various percussion instruments.

Group co-operation to put together the composition is another skill required for this project.

Notes and Inspiration

A Rondo for Rhythm Instruments

DAY I – INTRODUCTION TO QUESTION AND ANSWER

Give each child some type of percussion instrument – drums, tambourines, sticks, pencils on desks, whatever you have available.

Play a simple rhythm such as ta, ti ti, ta, ta. Have them count the beats as you play.

e.g. 1   2   3   4

      ta   ti ti   ta   ta   ♩♪♪♩♩

Now ask them to play any rhythm they want while you count to four.

Some children will inevitably go beyond the four beats. Therefore you must repeat this many times to make sure they stop on or before four beats. Make a game of this until everyone is silent after four beats.

Once this is accomplished, explain that what you, the teacher, played was the question and what they played was the answer. Questions and answers can change as long as you stay within the framework of the beat.

Now you are ready to do this over and over without a pause – first your question then their answer.

When this seems easy, ask for some volunteers to play the question and the whole class will answer. So far the answer is just a melange of sounds ending within the four-beat framework.

Next divide the children into twos and have each pair work together to create a question and an answer.

Maybe they can practise two or three sets in a row and then present them to the class. Those who need an extra challenge can be asked to create an introduction and an ending.

DAY 2 — CREATING THE A SECTION

You and the children create a question and answer section that all the children will play.

Here is an example in 4/4 time but you should create your own:

All drums play the question:

♪ ♪ ♩ ♪ ♪ ♪ ♩ | ♩ ♩ ♪ ♪ ♩

Everyone else answers: ♪ ♪ ♪ ♪ ♪ ♪ ♩ | ♩ ♩ ♩

Perhaps the children can work out their own in small groups and then you and the children can choose the best one to use for your rondo.

Once this is accomplished you can go on to day 4.

I have suggested an alternative day 2 and day 3 but this is not necessary to complete the rondo.

ALTERNATE DAY 2 — UNEVEN QUESTION AND ANSWER

If your students find question and answer easy, you might try this.

I have made a giant leap here, assuming that the children can easily respond to question and answer. I suggest making the question longer than the answer.

In 4/4 time, the question could be as follows:

>				>			
1	2	3	4	1	2	3	4
ta	ta	ta	ta	ta	ta	ta	ta

>	
1	2
ta	ta

The answer would fit in the remaining 6 beats; for example:

		>			
3	4	1	2	3	4
rest	ta	ta	ta	ta	ta

In musical notation it might look like this:

Question ♩ ♩ ♩ ♩ | ♩ ♩ ♩ ♩ | ♩ ♩

Answer   𝄾 | ♩ | ♩ ♩ ♩ ♩

You could try this word rhythm if you find it easier:

We are happy, We are hungry, Yum, Yum
(rest) It's time to eat now

with strong beats on We, We, Yum, and time.

This is easier than it seems on paper. The children will feel the beat and complete the answer very naturally. Be sure to put a strong beat on the first beat of each bar.

Once they can do this easily, have some members of the class play the question on some instrument of which you have several; drums are best but they are not always available.

Have other members of the class play the answer on a variety of miscellaneous instruments. (Kazoos, bicycle horns, train whistles, etc. make a nice addition to this activity.)

Do this many times until it seems very natural. Always keep the same rhythm for the question but encourage the students to vary the answers.

Sometimes the children will find it easier to do if you point out that the strong beats come on beat 1; therefore the answer is weak, strong, weak, weak, weak. Verbalize this only if you think it helps and the children can understand the concept. Otherwise keep the activity to a rhythmic reaction response.

Switch around the children playing the question and those playing the answer.

If you need to do more at this level, divide them into groups of four with at least one member of each group playing the question and the others playing the answer. The children may create wonderful answers involving more than one instrument.

ALTERNATE DAY 3 — ANSWERS IN DIFFERENT TIMBRES

Work again on the uneven question and answer. When the pattern is established divide the children into groups of three to six. (I always find that if there are too many children arguments arise.) Give each of the children in each group an instrument of a different timbre; for example, a triangle, a pair of sticks, a tambourine, a kazoo, a cymbal.

Ask them to create the answer on these five instruments with each instrument playing for one beat. This is not hard but they may take several runs at it before they can do it. It does take some co-operation, a skill in itself.

You, the teacher, should play the question and have each group in turn give you the answer. Some of the groups will be very inventive. Encourage them to use some eighth notes as well as quarter notes in the answer. There can be more than one instrument playing at a time. You can discuss which instrument works best at the very end and which on the strong beat or the word "time".

Now you can create a composition by playing this with all the groups in sequence: question–answer, question–answer, question–answer, until all groups have played.

Day 4 — CREATING THE B, C, D ETC. SECTIONS

What we have learned on the first three days makes the A section for a rondo. Today we will start work on the B section.

Divide the children into four groups.

Within these groups the children will create new questions and answers to last 16 beats. Encourage a B section that contrasts with the A section in its use of instruments and its rhythms. The question in the B section should not be similar to the A section. If the children fully understand question and answer, then let them work by themselves first before you try to guide them. Just make sure they know the correct number of beats they need in total. The time to make some suggestions is when they perform their creations.

Hint: Within each group you should have at least one instrument of the type that will play the question for the A section.

Working out these question and answers may take an entire class. Some will be better than others and class performances followed by discussion will raise the levels of all the groups. You might want to break more than once to show work in progress.

DAY 5 — COMBINING THE A AND B SECTIONS

Divide the children once again into four groups. They will probably need to review the A section to get their parts straight. Then review the B section so they have a plan for their turn.

One way to do this with a class of 30 children is to give about 10 children the instrument with which to play the question in the A section, drums in our example. Place two or three of these drummers in each one of the four groups. The children without the drums will play the answer for the A section. They can then use all the instruments in their group to create the B section for their group.

Now, have everyone in each group with the type of instrument selected for playing the question to the A section play this question. In our example it was drums but this is not necessary. The children in the first group will answer. Repeat this until all group have played their question and answers. Now the first group will play their entire B section.

Now repeat the A section from all groups and then the B section from the second group and so on until all have played. End with the A section.

If you have four groups you will end up with 16 bars of A section, four from each group and 4 bars from each B, C, D, and E group. The composition will be 80 bars in length. The explanation of this is much more difficult than the doing of it and the children love the accomplishment.

If you have four groups it will be like this:

Question A, group 1 answer; Question A, group 2 answer; Question A, group 3 answer; Question A, group 4 answer; B section from group 1

Question A, group 1 answer; Question A, group 2 answer; Question A, group 3 answer; Question A, group 4 answer; C section from group 2

Question A, group 1 answer; Question A, group 2 answer; Question A, group 3 answer; Question A, group 4 answer; D section from group 3

Question A, group 1 answer; Question A, group 2 answer; Question A, group 3 answer; Question A, group 4 answer; E section from group 4

Question A, group 1 answer; Question A, group 2 answer; Question A, group 3 answer; Question A, group 4 answer;

In shorter form:

A 1, 2, 3, 4, B
A 1, 2, 3, 4, C
A 1, 2, 3, 4, D
A 1, 2, 3, 4, E
A 1, 2, 3, 4.

They have now created a lengthy composition.

I have done this activity often with children in grades 4 and 5. I have also on occasion done this with children in grade 7 and 8.

Canon in Movement and Music

These lessons combine the musical form of canon or round with the same form in simple movements.

Concentration is required for a canon. Children are used to doing activities in unison, each one supporting the other. In a canon they are all doing the same thing but not at the same time. This requires independent thought and an ability to concentrate on their own activity while working alongside others. These lessons will deal with both playing the instruments in canon and moving in canon – an activity most children delight in. It becomes a game – something all children enjoy.

Learning the movement in canon helps to solidify the form in the child's mind. It leads the way to co-ordinating music with movement and it shows how the whole body can be used to express an idea.

Technically, these lessons emphasize the C major scale. Many pieces for children use the five-note pentatonic scale, but this one uses a seven-note scale. This bit of theory can be explored or ignored at this point depending on the classroom requirements.

This piece also uses the technical ability to play hand over hand on the instruments. This can be very hard for some students and will require some extra time in most classrooms. This type of skill development can be very important in all academic endeavours.

Notes and Inspiration

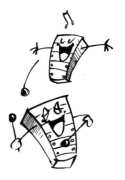

Canon in Movement and Music

DAY 1 – LEARNING TO BE AN ECHO

Echo clapping

Start with echo sounds of patsching, snapping fingers, clapping and stamping. You will be the leader, and for ease of management stick to beats of four.

e.g. 1. patsch, patsch, clap, clap – the children repeat
2. clap clap, snap, snap – the children repeat etc.

or for use with younger children who find it easier to end with a rest:

e.g. 1. patsch, patsch, clap, rest – the children repeat
2. clap clap, snap, rest – the children repeat etc.

You can carry this on as long as you like, making the patterns increasingly difficult. Eighth notes can of course be mixed with quarter and half notes.

The order of the body percussion

You will find as you give them these patterns to repeat that the order is a large factor in their difficulty. If you do them straight down the body, i.e. snap, clap, patsch, stamp, more of the children will follow you exactly than if you clap, stamp, snap, patsch. This order is much harder for the children to follow quickly. On the other hand it does provide a challenge to the experts.

As long as you realize this, you can try some patterns in other orders so that the children can see the difference in difficulty. I would explain this to them after many examples. Perhaps you could ask them to explain why one is harder than the other. **This is necessary because in the end the students will be the leaders.**

You could even at this point experiment with several different children as leaders for this mirroring or echo clapping.

Now add movement

Having accomplished this you can add other movements to your rhythms – change of levels, greater arm movements, leg movements and so on.

I encourage you to try these simple movements with the children even if you are not comfortable with dance. The children will lead you through them because they are not afraid to move. You simply have to keep them from losing focus. Have them be the leaders if you feel insecure about this.

The length of time you spend on this depends greatly on the past experience of the children. If this is their first attempt at this, then these suggestions for day 1 might in fact take you into day 2 and day 3 before going on to the rest of the suggestions. If you have done a lot of echo clapping, then the movement will be accomplished probably on the first day.

DAY 2 – MOVEMENT AS ECHO AND CANON

Echo clapping and movement with a partner

Review the movement and echo clapping and then have the children form pairs. One group may have to be a three. Ask them to choose one child in each group to be number one and one (or two) to be number two. Number one becomes the leader and will present four beats of echo clapping to their partner, who will then echo it back.

As the teacher I play the piano to give a steady rhythm but you can play anything that will provide a strong rhythm such as a drum or tambourine.

After a minute or so ask the number two partner to be the leader. Once they do this easily with the clapping and patching, encourage them to perform these movements while using the various levels available – stretching up high, crouching down low, etc. *Note: It is not a good idea to lie down as it is hard to do this in time to the rhythm.*

The next step – body percussion canon

Once they have accomplished this, you again become the leader. This time you will try the same thing in canon. Start very simply so they understand the concept.

You will clap for four beats and snap for four beats. While you are snapping they will be asked to clap the four beats you started with. As you go on clapping for four beats they will be snapping for four; then you can patsch for four while they snap for four. Children catch on to this very quickly but it may take a couple of explanations for the whole class to get the idea.

Here is an example:

Bar			
1	2	3	4

Leader			
clap, clap, clap, clap,	snap, snap, snap, snap,	clap, clap, clap, clap,	patsch, patsch, patsch, patsch

Children			
silence,	clap, clap, clap, clap,	snap, snap, snap, snap,	clap, clap, clap, clap,

Large body movements in canon

You can try different movements of this type, then add the whole body movements and levels as you did with the echoing.

Hint: Try a couple of movements where you actually turn around. They will see and experience that this does not work because they cannot concentrate on your next movement unless they are watching you.

A simple example:

Bar			
1	2	3	4

Leader			
arms, arms, arms, arms,	crouch, crouch, crouch, crouch,	wave, wave, wave, wave,	head, head, head, head

Children			
silence,	arms, arms, arms, arms,	crouch, crouch, crouch, crouch,	wave, wave, wave, wave

DAY 3 – CREATING THEIR OWN CANON MOVEMENTS

Have the children form partners and try movements in canon as you did with them at the end of the last class. Once again, accompany their movements with music or rhythm. Stop the class every few minutes to have one set of partners show what they are doing. If you think it is wise, change the partners and have children work with new partners.

Then make the groups into fours and have the movement go around the group one at a time so the canon is now in four. They must watch only the child they must follow. Some are much better at this than others. Choose a group that is good and have the class watch. Try not to be critical but merely encouraging.

Ask them to make up a small pattern for a 30-second performance. If some groups develop a pattern immediately while others are still working, then ask those who are finished to add an introduction and an ending perhaps in unison. Children for the most part love doing little productions of their own.

DAY 4 (OPTIONAL) – MAKING IT A GAME

I have done this more as a time filler than a class but I mention it here because the children really seem to enjoy this. Make the groups first of four and have them practice movement in canon. You will be wise to make them choose the leader before they start and also the order of who follows who. I suggest having them raise their hands at the beginning to show who is number 1, number 2, number 3, number 4. This ends the arguments.

Next have them make groups of eight and do the same thing and try to keep the movement going around the circle. This is akin to playing telephone. You must concentrate on the person from whom you are receiving the movement and no-one else.

If they can do it in eights, then try sixteen and eventually the whole class. This makes a very good exercise for a hot June day.

PACHELBEL'S CANON

DAY 5 — TIME TO LEARN THE MUSIC

Pachelbel's Canon

This piece simplified for Orff is basically a major scale. As such it makes a good piece for singing the notes of the scale whether by letter names or by tonic solfege.

You can sing the tune on the opposite page as

CDEFGABCC, EDCBAGFEE, CBAGFEDCC. The underlined notes are the eighth notes.

This of course gets the note spelling alphabet going in both directions, something many children find a challenge.

Alternatively

do, re, mi, fa, so, la, ti, do, do

mi, re, do, ti, la, so, fa, mi, mi

do, ti, la, so, fa, mi, re, do, do

The underlined notes are of course eighth notes. So it can be sung

ta, ti-ti, ta, ta, ta, ta, ta, ta ;

ta, ta, ta, ta, ti-ti, ta, ta, ta;

ta, ta, ta, ta, ti-ti, ta, ta, ta;

This can then be transferred to the instruments. If previous music has all been in the pentatonic scale, this will provide an entire new learning situation. You can use the opportunity to discuss the C major scale.

This song should be played hand over hand going up and down the instrument. I would learn two bars at a time and work on this until it is easy. It can be played on all the instruments at the same time, percussion and recorders if you wish.

Depending on the ability and experience of our class this exercise may be handled in one day or on several days. Go as slowly as is necessary to get a satisfactory sound.

DAY 6 — PLAYING THE MUSIC IN CANON

Review the notes in unison and then add the ostinato bass line with whatever instrument you wish. If you do not have a bass xylophone, then experiment with other instruments while the melody is being played. Let the children decide which they want to use and why.

Bass or ostinato part:

CGAEFEDCC *or*

do, so, la, mi, fa, mi, re, do, do *or*

ta, ta, ta, ta, ti-ti ta, ta, ta.

Choose a child or children who can keep a steady beat for this part.

Hint: Always put a strong musician on the bass part. It will hold the whole thing together.

Now for the canon

It is very effective if each part of the canon is played by a different instrument. For example, try part 1 on the soprano xylophones, part 2 on the alto xylophones, part 3 on the glockenspiels. Each set of instruments will start two bars apart as the music shows and the ostinato plays throughout.

Experiment with the children to decide which instrument should start the piece. They will have their own ideas.

Optional: Metallophones are not good instruments for this piece as they muddy both parts. You can, however, have them play the sound of bells in the background: A and E

together. This dissonance gives a lovely sound of church bells off in the distance. See the music. This is not necessary unless you need to use the metallophones.

Once the children are good at this piece as a class, divide them up into groups of four to play the music by themselves. They will enjoy these solo performances. Once again, try not be critical of those who have difficulty but rather emphasize the excellent effort.

DAY 7 — MUSIC AND MOVEMENT TOGETHER

Music and movement in canon

Choose some children to play the instruments, and the rest divide into groups of three.

Explain that the movement of the first person will be alone for two bars, or eight beats, whichever is the easiest for them to understand. This might be walking or arm circling for eight beats.

The second person will echo or mirror the movement with which the first person started but will not start this until the second instrument starts. The third person will do the first movement when the third instrument starts. As they did earlier in exploring movement in canon, the first person will create a new section once the second has started and another new section for the third time. They must keep the movement simple if it is to be noted and remembered by the follower while the follower is doing the first movement. Make sure the leader never creates a movement where he/she turns around. The follower could get completely lost.

Let them try this with the music. Do not be surprised if you have to do this beginning stage several times before everyone understands. Have one group give a demonstration.

You can do this in many ways – first switching the leaders and followers, and, as well, switch the players and the children doing the movement, thus giving everyone a chance to play and to do movement.

If you have enough instruments, break up into smaller groups and work out individual routines that satisfy the canon. Some children will always want to play while others will always want to move.

This could easily take more than one day to accomplish. Try not to become frustrated if it is a bit chaotic. I have found that as soon as one group accomplishes the movement canon with the music, the rest will quickly follow.

DAY 8 – MOVEMENT TO INTERPRET THE MUSIC

Divide the children into groups of four to six. My preference is to have boys and girls working together in groups so I usually say that every group must have at least one member of each sex. This usually divides them pretty evenly.

Now they know the music, ask them to create a smoother set of movements to describe each section of music. You should discuss the reason for this – that this is a quiet gentle piece of music requiring a similar appropriate type of interpretation. In other areas this might be called a dance but I would refrain from using this word at this point unless your children have had a lot of training in creative movement. You may have to give them samples of the type of movement that would work but do not give them too much. They are much more creative than most adults and you do not want them restricted by your movements.

As they are working, if you see a good set of movements developing, stop the class and point this out.

I find that as a bonus to developing the movement you will hear the children singing the piece in canon with no prompting from you.

This part of the project can be worked on for one day or several days depending on where you want it to go.

DAY 9, ETC. – AN ENTIRE PRODUCTION

If you want to carry this further, here are some suggestions:

You can join different groups of work together to create a lengthened choreography.

You can, along with the children, develop an introduction and an ending.

The canon can be played over and over again with different instruments picking up the various parts and the movement using these changes.

You could combine all of these into an entire production *or* you can just stop anywhere along the chain of things when you have accomplished your goal for this particular set of lessons.

Lummi Sticks

This is a game which children of all ages can enjoy. In fact, I learned about these sticks first at a high school dance, where everyone sat with their partner and tried these patterns. Needless to say, high school dances have changed.

This game requires good eye-hand co-ordination and this is a skill worth developing for academics and the arts.

We explore various rhythm patterns and work out stick routines to fit them. The children learn to create their own and to make the form fit with the pattern of a given chant. Once they can pass the sticks easily and they have learned the patterns, the children can add them to large-muscle movements, "dances", to create very interesting patterns. You will find all children enjoy these games.

Notes and Inspiration

Lummi Sticks

Playing with lummi sticks was originally a New Zealand children's game. It is a lot of fun and most children can master it and enjoy the concentration involved.

Equipment

You need two lummi sticks per child, each lummi stick being 1 foot (30 cm) long and made out of 1-inch doweling. It is a good idea to sand the sticks before using them to keep splinters to a minimum. I inherited a set of sticks that someone had varnished. They certainly tend to last longer that way but varnish is not essential.

Each child that is playing needs two sticks, and two children make a set. Sometimes when I am introducing lummi sticks and the children are a bit excited, I give the sticks to every second set and the others watch until it is their turn. This keeps the noise down and is often a good idea because one set of children can see what the others do and eagerly wait their turn to try to do better.

Formation

The best formation is a longways set – two long rows sitting cross-legged facing each other, the person opposite being the partner. Obviously the rows can snake around the room where necessary. I will explain later how I deal with an uneven number of children

LONGWAYS SET

DAY 1 – SIMPLE PASSING OF THE STICK

Once you have explained the formation to the children, they should sit down in their rows. Hand out one lummi stick to each child. Show them how to hold the sticks, upright, vertical not horizontal. Start out with one stick in each right hand. The children should put their left hands behind their backs.

Now, pass the stick to your partner. Obviously there is a problem because the other person has a stick in the hand to which you are trying to pass. Thus, you must let go and grab the other stick. If these were adults you were instructing, you could tell them to throw the stick gently, but *throw* seems to make children lose their focus. If you explain that you are gently passing the stick it seems to work better.

The rows should be quite close together so that the distance to pass the stick is not very far – knees of partners almost touching.

Hint: This basic lummi stick skill is not hard to learn but I recommend that you try it with a friend before you try to teach it. I would not try this below the age of 7 and with children this young I recommend simply sitting in a circle and passing the stick in time to music before attempting the above partner work. I have used the lummi sticks mostly with children ages 9 – 13.

Now you must explain to the children that the stick must go straight ahead of the person holding it while he/she reaches out to grab the stick of the partner. You cannot pass on a diagonal or the sticks will collide.

The children can practise this for five or ten minutes depending on the discipline. If they become very silly the game can become dangerous. **They must watch the stick of the other person, not their own.** This will avoid any accidents with eyes. About every minute or so, stop everyone and have two children demonstrate the pattern alone for the class to see and to comment on their progress.

After five or ten minutes it is good idea to change partners. Some children learn this skill more quickly than others and a change helps to spread the expertise around. One way to change is to tell everyone with their backs to the window to stand up and move two people to the left (or right or whatever) and if there is a child without a partner this child can now join the rotation and have a partner and another child in line will be without a partner until they again make a change.

After changing partners, try the same basic skill again. This is a good point at which to try passing the stick with the left hand, while holding the right hand behind the back. Stress again that you are merely passing the stick, not tossing it in the air, that it must go straight ahead, not on a diagonal, and that you must watch the partner's stick.

Change partners again and try with sticks in both hands. You can alternate pairs with and without sticks or give out more sticks so that each child has two.

A good pattern to start with is:

Tap sticks on the knees for one,
Click together for two,
Exchange right-hand sticks for three,
Click together for four.

Then repeat with the *left* hands.
Tap sticks on the knees for one,
Click together for two,
Exchange left-hand sticks for three,
Click together for four.

The children can chant: *Knees, click, right, click, Knees, click, left, click.*

One thing to stress is **always watch your partner's stick, not your own. That way you will not get hurt when a pass goes astray.**

Don't be discouraged by a lot of sticks rolling around on the floor as the catching is not too accurate at first. The children will get better at catching them but it could take at least four half-hour classes.

Hint: The first beat could be on the floor instead of on the knees if noise throughout the rest of the building is not a problem. Thirty children hitting the floor at once with a stick echoes a long way within a school.

This is a good stopping place for day 1.

DAY 2 – PASSING PATTERNS

Review the activities of day 1 and try some of the new patterns even if the co-ordination is not yet perfect.

Set up the longways set and give out the sticks. Start with the pattern you ended with on the first day. You will have to emphasize again and again that:

1. the sticks must go straight across,
2. you watch your partner's stick, not your own
3. you are gently passing the stick, not heaving it at your partner.

You can probably use some of the children to demonstrate. While the whole class is working at this pattern, I usually play something on the piano to keep them in time. You could also do this on a drum or any other instrument loud enough to be heard. It helps to keep the whole group together. Sticks will roll around the floor while this is happening and I just let the children get their sticks back while the others continue. They can pick up the rhythm when they are ready. Once again, I recommend changing partners quite frequently.

A contest: Start everyone together and see which pair can keep going the longest without dropping a stick. You have to watch the cheating on this one. Sometimes the child without the partner can watch for this.

Some may worry that this shows up the weak child but in my experience most of the class drop the sticks within the first two cycles and we end up with two or three sets of partners battling it out for 5 or 6 cycles. It is interesting to note that sometimes a child who is not good at the other parts of the program is excellent at this, and thus winning one of these contests lasting about a minute is a real morale builder. I have also had experience with some children who are excellent orchestral players but could not master the lummi stick game without a great deal of effort. So in its way, it is a great equalizer in the classroom.

A new move – flipping the stick: Point both sticks to the floor, tap gently and flip the sticks in toward you and catch them after one flip (half a rotation). Most children can do this easily but some will have trouble understanding the concept. Once this skill is mastered you can add it to the pattern.

A new pattern

Possible new chant:

Knees, click, down, flip,
Knees, click, right, click
Knees, click, down flip,
Knees, click, left, click

This pattern together with changing partners and contests will occupy the class for half an hour. If they seem to be getting good at it and need a challenge, ask them to develop a new pattern using the same moves. It is often interesting to see what they think of.

DAY 3, 4, 5 – INCREASING THE SKILL

New Patterns – Peripheral vision

This could be the next day, next week or many weeks away.

A different flip: The same type of flip but this time, one on each side of you simultaneously. This is harder as you cannot see both sticks and have to trust to your spatial feeling.

Two sticks at once: Passing two sticks at once provides new problems; one partner must pass outside, the other inside, and they must decide which before they begin.

Once this is mastered you can try a pattern such as this:

Chant

Knees, click, right, click, (pass with the right)
Knees click left click, (pass with the left)
Knees click both click, (pass both together)
Down flip, down, flip etc. (point down and flip twice

Once again with the new moves, try changing partners, holding contests and finally having the children create their own patterns. They may want to try certain moves while standing up and they might create introductions and endings.

EXTENDED LESSONS

A new rhythm

This gives you a mixed-meter rhythm ,

Say

1	2	3,	1	2	3,	1	2	1	2;
1	2	3,	1	2	3,	1	2	1	2

Concentrate, concentrate, don't you drop them
Concentrate, concentrate, don't you drop them
Knees click right, knees click left, down flip, down flip
Knees click right, knees click left, down flip, down flip

Different size groups: Have the children make groups of four or five where necessary and ask them to make up some passing patterns. Use the rhythm of their names as a chant or make up a poem or some counting game. If they become good at this, ask them to create an introduction and an ending. Maybe they can change levels while doing this – that is, stand up or walk around.

I once used this type of exercise as a way of describing some very stylized art work. We ended up putting coloured ribbons on the sticks to portray the art and the rhythms the children created expressed how they felt about the art.

Memorizing facts – integration of arts and academics

You can use chanting while playing with the lummi sticks as a way of memorizing math formulae and multiplication facts. It could be the basis for some poetry assignment. Someone once used these rhythm sticks to interpret the chorus in a Greek tragedy. Once the skill is learned, the possibilities are endless. Have some idea where you want the process to go but then let the children lead you through their ideas.

As an example, here are some chants for math formulae:

Right ring, left ring
$2\pi r$ is the outside ring.

•

Right click toss with a
Partner I'm paired, the
Area of a circle is
πr squared.

•

Round the outside ring we go
$\pi d \quad \pi d$
The distance round the circle is
πd – now we're home.

Colours of the Rainbow

In the development of language arts it is necessary to learn to communicate in many different ways. This lesson starts with an outline of free verse and asks the students to describe how colours affect them and their activities.

They are asked first to state simple ideas and then, using examples with adjective and adverb phrases and clauses, to extend these ideas to create small drama scenes.

Having created these ideas, the children can then learn to expand their ideas with actions and sound effects.

A discussion of the colours of a rainbow is a side effect to these lessons.

The music in this set of lessons is based on a different scale. It is neither the pentatonic or C major scale presented earlier. This exploration of yet another music outline all adds to the child's knowledge of music.

This particular set of lessons can be used with any age group from 7 to 14. The results will be very different but from my experience, they all love the ideas.

Notes and Inspiration

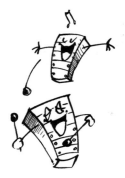

Colours of the Rainbow

DAY 1 — START WITH A BLANK POEM

Here is a suggestion for a starting outline.

_____ is _____

It _____ and it

_____

It does_____

It is _____.

This is merely the starting point but gives the children some structure from which to begin.

The first word must be a colour and since we are discussing a rainbow (for purposes of integration with perhaps science or art) we will use only the basic colours of a rainbow – red, orange, yellow, green, blue and purple – and if you want you can add black and white to describe the colours of a storm that often accompanies a rainbow.

I will give an example of how they might start, but the children are usually much more creative than I.

Note: The wording of my example does not follow the outline exactly. That is not important. The outline is to give them a starting place.

Red is the colour of a fire engine
It is the colour of the snow fence at the bottom of the hill
It makes me stop at street corners and flashes when a train is crossing
Red is the colour of my favourite hat.

This is where the children will start, and working in groups of two or three it will take at least one class of 30 to 40 minutes to get this far.

DAY 2 — EXPANDING THE POEM

Having kept copies of the first creations, I find it useful to have the children stretch their poems. I will give you an example of what I look for.

Red is the colour of a fire engine that I chased down the street and because I wasn't looking I fell into a puddle.

It is the colour of the snow fence at the bottom of the hill to keep us all from sliding into the lake.

It makes me stop at street corners so I won't hit pedestrians when I am riding my shiny new red bike and it flashes on a little country road late at night to tell me when a train is coming.

Red is the colour of my favourite hat that I try to wear to dinner when my Mom isn't looking.

This may take two or three more classes. I suggest a lot of sharing before you and the children get what they want from these poems.

DAY 3 AND DAY 4 — STRETCHING AND REFINING

When they are stretching these poems, you should keep in mind that the end result of these poems is some drama.

Some things are hard to dramatize; for example, *Red is the colour of the text book I hate.* This becomes easier to dramatize if it is *Red is the colour of the text book with the math problems that I had to stay up all night to finish.*

Hint: I try to give them ideas using colours other than the colour with which they are working. Then the tendency to copy exactly what I say is not so strong.

Try to not become frustrated. Have the children write down their creations, share them with the class and then improve them even more. This will take several periods. I think it is better to have it go over several periods than all on one day. It allows time for creative thought. When they think they are finished and you are not so sure, ask them how they would dramatize their little poems.

DAY 5 AND DAY 6 – WORK OUT THE DRAMAS

Time to try to work out the drama or actions that will tell the story of the poem.

If you were working on the math textbook above, there might be a little dialogue with Mother telling the student he or she should be in bed while the student knows the homework must be finished. The student could be seen wrestling with the math problem and agonizing over not getting the required answer.

In groups of three or four it can take a long time dealing with all four lines of the poem.

DAY 7 AND 8 – ADD SOUND EFFECTS

Now that they have worked out some drama ideas, it is useful to allow them at least one percussion instrument for sound effects. If you have never discussed the various timbres and uses of the percussion instruments, you should spend at least one class on this at this time before expecting the students to use these instruments effectively.

(If your children have had this type of experience then go on to day 9. You might prefer to do this exploration as a unit by itself or just before starting a project like colours.)

Exploring percussion instruments

If your children have never experimented with percussion sounds, this is one way to discover that percussion instruments can make many different sounds, not just the ones originally expected from them. I hand out hand drums, cymbals, cow bells, claves, etc. Then I hand out cards on which each has a different design. The design suggests a type of sound pattern – loud and sharp, dotted and far spaced, spiral, etc. Each child is asked to produce the sound on the card with the particular instrument she or he has. We talk about the effect and then switch cards. Then we obviously switch instruments. For example, there are many ways to play a drum. You can beat it with a beater, beat it with your hand, rub it with your hand or rub it with paper, hit it hard in the centre to get a dead sound or make the sound of raindrops with your fingernails. Every instrument has a similar range of possibilities.

Follow the same procedure with the melodic Orff instruments. Discuss the different ways these instruments can enhance your presentations. It is not always necessary to use the mallets in the conventional fashion – e.g. the handles often make interesting sounds for different purposes.

SAMPLES OF CARDS

for percussion experiments.

 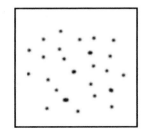  

DAY 9 — ADD THE SOUND EFFECTS TO THE DRAMAS

Now it is time to enhance the dramas with these sounds. The groups can play for each other if everyone in the group is needed for the presentations.

DAY 10 — HOW TO JOIN THE POEMS TOGETHER

Time to work out a way to join the poems together if you want a complete presentation.

You can use a song to join these, or I have sometimes used the sound effects of a storm – thunder, lightning, etc. You can make good thunder sounds by using a piece of sheet metal and shaking it. You might want to use the black and white poems for joining together the other colour poems. It depends on what has developed.

Note: You can obviously use the beginning outline with any colours and proceed on subjects other than a rainbow. For example, you could develop a theme based on summer fun. You could use this method to interpret a story you've just read in language arts. Or you can do the poems in isolation simply as a language arts project.

DAY 11 — LEARN A SONG

Colour Me A Rainbow

This piece is basically in the E-E or phrygian mode with an occasional switch into E major with the G#. This G# is a key many Orff instruments do not have so leave it out if you do not have it. Do not substitute G natural for G sharp.

1. Learn the tune and the words.

2. Add the bass line.

3. The xylophone and metallophone parts can be played on any instrument.

Work on one line at a time. Line three is the same as line one except for the last note. The glockenspiel part is decoration to be added last.

The eighth notes in line two can be played by glockenspiels or xylophones. Experiment with the instrumentation and change it as you see fit. It is a good idea to play it in many different ways with the children and then have them give their opinion as to which instrument is best on which part and why.

Hint: When I did this with a class we made a simple dance to this music and used surveyor's tape as coloured ribbon to enhance the dance. This tape, available in hardware stores, comes in brilliant colours and is very inexpensive.

DAY 12 ETC. — CREATING A PERFORMANCE

Now you can put all these elements together to make a performance. One suggested order is (a) song, (b) colour poems divided by stormy sounds and then (a) the song when the storm is over. Experiment with other ideas.

COLOUR ME A RAINBOW

Words and Music Alice Brass

The higher notes, marked 8ve, to be played on a soprano glockenspiel, the lower notes on an alto glockenspiel.

Glockenspiels (sop. and alto)

Xylophones or metallophones

Xylophones or metallophones

Bass

Colour me a rain -bow   All the hues.   Col-our me a rain - bow   Tur-quoise   blue

Yel-low turns to orange and red   Pur-ple with some blue can meet.   Green goes back to yel-low then the cy- cle   is com- plete.

Col-our me a rain - bow   Let me see   All the ma - ny col - ours   that may be.

Improvisation

Children love it so have courage and try it.

There is a great mystique about improvisation but it simply means to make up something.

I am often asked how I get the children to improvise. I am more likely to ask the question, **how do you get children to stop improvising?**

Children love to make up their own thing – be it a game, a drawing, a new dessert or a piece of music. If you give them some simple parameters with which to create and harmonize melodies, they come up with the most amazing and wonderful creations.

First they must have some skills in using the instruments. I am always aware that children need to feel safe to improvise, so I always start with ways they can hide their experiments at first. Later, when they are proud of what they are doing, they want to show you and their peers.

In these three projects, intended to be done in order, the children will progress from simple two-bar creations to entire tunes written to enhance a poem. We in fact turn improvisation into composing as we experiment with ideas that are specific to music structure.

Notes and Inspiration

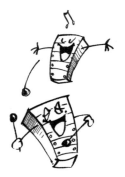

Improvisation 1
For Beginners

Feeling safe and experimenting with sound

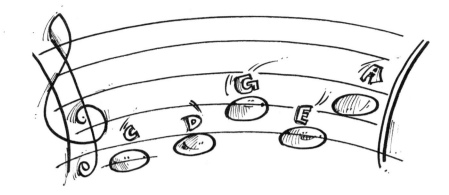

Day 1 – Exploring the Pentatonic Scale

Playing what you want within the pentatonic scale

As soon as the children feel comfortable holding the mallets and getting a sound out of the instruments, you can let them play what they want – i.e., improvise. Ask them to take the B's and F's (the burgers and fries) off the instruments, being careful to reach across the instruments so as not to bend the nails. (One teacher I heard said, "Lift straight off like a helicopter not at an angle like an airplane.") This should be done with all the instruments in the Orff orchestra.

Explain to them that you will count to four, they will play for four beats, and then be silent again while you count to four again, and so on. They can play anything they want in that four-beat time period but then they must be silent for the second four beats. Because the instruments are set up on a pentatonic scale, the effect will be tolerable even with 30 instruments (for those of you who are lucky enough to have a class set of instruments). You will find at the beginning that **the silence is the hardest**. If all the children cannot learn to be silent for those four beats, then I suggest you try two or three children at a time until everyone gets the idea.

First restriction

Once they play for four and are silent for four you can go on to the next step. Ask them to play only one note at a time and to alternate hands as they do this. Most of the children will play one note to a beat when asked to play one note at a time. From this you can then ask them to perhaps add some running notes or ti-ti notes or whatever you know they will understand. Rest spaces are OK too. You might pick out some volunteers to play their solo four-beat creations if you think this will help the other children.

A bit of form

Next you can ask the glockenspiels to play on the first four beats, the soprano xylophones on the next four, alto xylophones the next four and so on. Once this is accomplished, some child can play an underlying ostinato rhythm on a drum, or the bass if you have one. For example: if you use a bass simply play C G on beat 1 and 3 while the groups play, one by one, their four-beat section with a rest for four beats between groups. Remember, the children are still playing their own choice of notes but only for four beats.

DAY 2 – QUESTION AND ANSWER

What makes a good melody – the beginning of question and answer

I would place the children in a circle for today's lesson. Once again, set up the C pentatonic scale (no B's of F's). **Review the last class first.** Now, ask them all to play for both four-beat sections with one restriction. At the end of the first four-beat section, do not end on C. On the last four-beat section they must end on C. Follow the same plan as day 1; that is, once all the instruments can do this together have the glockenspiels play alone, then the soprano xylophones alone, and so on. You will want to omit the 4 silent beats to keep the music flowing. Do this as soon as you think the children are able.

An accompanying ostinato

As soon as this seems comfortable, have some instrument play the basic rhythm, i.e. C G, on beat one and three or if they are able, C G A G on beats one to four. This ostinato could also be done with a drum or wood block, or if you feel so inclined all three at once.

Then, with the underlying part established, proceed around the circle having each child play four beats – the first child ending on anything but C, the second child on ending on C. They will hear that they have created little melodies.

What makes a good melody?

You can then discuss the fact that most really good melodies move by steps, not huge leaps. *Doe, A Deer* is a good example for children, as is *Mary and her lamb*. You can find many other good examples from your experience or ask the children to suggest some.

Now try the circle again praising the really good attempts at flowing melodies.

Play both the question and the answer

Next, each child can play both four-beat sections ending the first one on any note but C while the second one must end on C. (Note: they have eliminated the four beats of silence.)

In this exercise the children have created a musical question and a musical answer, similar to the rhythmic question and answer created in the lesson on Rondo.

DAY 3 – RHYTHMIC QUESTION AND ANSWER

(This is similar to what we did in *Rondo for Rhythm Instruments* earlier in this book. You can probably skip this day if you have covered the rondo in detail.)

Start this class with a clapping exercise or body percussion exercise. You clap four beats or eight beats to the children and they must answer with their own four or eight beats. At first do this with everyone together. This allows safe experimentation – i.e., nobody can hear what any one child is playing. Proper instrument technique must be stressed here. (*Note: Because they are all using the pentatonic scale, the sound of the whole group will be quite pleasant and each child will feel that what he or she is playing is acceptable. This gives them the confidence to play by themselves when their turn comes.*)

Once they seem to feel comfortable, ask for solo answers to your rhythmic questions. Talk about the best answers in relation to the question you asked. The answer will have some relationship to the question – it will repeat some of the parts, use the same body percussion, etc.

Ask the children to work in pairs, creating rhythmic question and answers that seem to go together.

Once this is accomplished put two pairs together and ask one pair to clap the underlying ostinato rhythm while the other pair improvises a pattern. They can then switch. Put the whole thing together and you have a piece of rhythmic music.

Always end classes such as this with at least ten minutes of showing what has been accomplished. Even if only one group is really good, it is worthwhile for all the children to show what they have created and to see the work of the others.

DAY 4 AND DAY 5 – INSTRUMENTAL QUESTION AND ANSWER

Repeat day 3 but using melodic instruments this time. Review what was done on day 1, day 2 and day 3. This time you will have some wonderful melodic patterns created by the children. It will take at least 15 minutes of total cacophony for these melodies to result but you should let them experiment with each other in groups of two or four before you ask them to play for the class. They must be allowed to work amongst themselves – you've had your input over the past couple of classes, now it is their turn. They will work for about 15 minutes, but then I find concentration goes and unfocused noise erupts.

Demonstration and comments from peers can end the class. This exercise can easily fill two half-hour periods or more if you feel it is needed.

My experience with this is that the children greatly enjoy making their own music but you must keep their work periods very short.

Notes and Inspiration

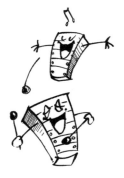

Improvisation 2
Melodies in Modes

For those who feel safe experimenting with music

GENERAL ADVICE

Be sure that a feeling of safety in creativity has been established by an exercise such as Improvisation 1. The children should have some confidence in simple improvisation before they are asked to try anything complicated. The keyword is *confidence*. They must feel sure they will accomplish something useful or they will not concentrate on the task at hand.

As well, the children should have some experience with pieces in different scales. You can give an example of something they learned and point out that it was built on a pentatonic scale, or a dorian mode, or an aeolian mode, or whatever. They will hear the different moods created by the different modes.

Note: 'Land of the Silver Birch' in this book is in the dorian mode. Another example of this mode is the folk song, 'She's like a Swallow'. A lot of country music is written in a pentatonic scale; one example is a piece called 'Buttons and Bows'.

DAY 1 — DORIAN MODE

A review of question and answer

Play a dorian scale on the instruments: D – D with no sharps and flats. Talk about what is unexpected about this scale: i.e., the flattened third and seventh compared to the major scale to which they are more accustomed. If some of your students know about minor scales, you can compare this scale to the dorian as well. Establish that the flattened seventh, C natural, must be present in order to establish the mode.

Talk about question and answer with the dorian mode. The question must end on any note but D and the answer must end on D. Having presented this, ask the students, "On what note will the question end and on what note will the answer end?" Again stress that the C makes a very good penultimate or second-last note to establish the key. It truly gives the piece its dorian feel.

Again in a circle (see Improvisation 1 for beginners), play question and answer around the circle, this time in the dorian mode. You might also discuss the mood this music creates.

A bass or other low instrument can play: D rest, F rest, as an ostinato to add interest to the music.

Once again, concentrate on the successes not the problems. You want the children to feel very comfortable.

Expand on the music

From here on let's try something different. You the teacher create a dorian tune with four bars of music and perhaps as many as three underlying parts or perhaps only one. I have given you an example but you really should try to create one yourself. Your creation will help you to help the children with theirs. These parts should be something that can be taught and learned easily and quickly. In other words, keep it simple.

The children are not restricted by harmony rules when they create an accompanying ostinato. They simply play what sounds terrific to them.

Once they have learned this, each child can now make up four bars to come in between each entry of the tune. You now have a rondo, with the tune as the A section and each child's improvisation as the various B, C, D and so on sections.

The only restrictions are:

1. Melody must move mostly by step.

2. Start on D, end on D (the start is not absolutely necessary but it seems to work best for the children).

3. Play or rest for the duration of 4 bars or 16 beats.

At least one ostinato part from the A section, probably the bass, can remain playing with each new 4-bar melody to hold the music together.

Classroom set up

I find it best to simply go around the circle without breaking the rhythm. If one child does not play anything for the first 8 beats, that was simply a rest. If you don't break the rhythm and the children can see what is happening, I find that the next time you go around they will all play. Try to start with some confident children. Confidence is all it takes as you have so few restrictions.

Dorian question - example

Soprano Xylophone

Glock

Xylophone

Bass

DAY 2 – OTHER MODES AND OTHER MOODS

Aeolian mode

Try the same thing in the aeolian mode A – A no accidentals. If the children become good at this and you need more activities in day 2 you can break into groups and see what they can create in this mode by themselves. You will be astonished at the results.

Depending on your situation, you can discuss the different moods created by the different modes. If you as the teacher have little experience with these modes, I encourage you to experiment on your own with them to get the feel for their various flavours.

I have had groups of children combine the aeolian mode with the dorian mode creating an ABA type of music. They were thrilled with their results.

DAY 3 – MORE MODES

I would definitely try the **mixolydian mode:** G – G with no F#. This creates a very jazzy feel which delights children. Follow the same format as day 1 and day 2. Talk about the different feeling each mode gives. Follow the plan of day 1 and day 2.

If you want to give the children a simple example of mixolydian, simply play

GG BB GG <u>D</u> GG FF <u>G</u>

in straight quarter note time except for the two underlined notes that are half notes.

DAY 4 – CREATING OSTINATOS

Creating ostinato parts – first using C pentatonic

Play with many different ostinato rhythms. Children need some help in creating underlying rhythms.

Examples (see below):

1 & 1A: Let's assume we are in C pentatonic. You can start with the simple rhythm of the strong beat played on the tonic or octave tonic notes on beats one and three.

2: Tonic, fifth, sixth, fifth or CGAG on every beat.

3: CAG with A being held for beat 2 and 3

4: CGGG with the second G an octave lower than the first and third G

5: CGGAG with the first G on the second half of the first beat and the second G on the second half of the second beat.

Next comes the fun part – ask the children for their suggestions. Some will work and some will not. Be prepared to discuss their ideas with them.

Try some improvisations in C pentatonic over some of these ostinatos and discuss which work the best. This may take an extra day all by itself.

DAY 5 – OSTINATOS IN THE MODES

Try some similar ostinatos in some of the modes. Experiment with them either as a class or in groups. If time permits, try adding some *decorations* on the glockenspiels; these could be glissandos, quick notes at phrase ends and so on. Then try improvising some modal melodies over these ostinatos and talk about the kind of music you have created.

Choice of instrument for each part

This could bring on discussion of which instrument is best for each part of the music. This of course differs with the piece. I have assumed in this particular case that the xylophones will probably play the melody but it could be played by the glockenspiels.

The metallophones create quite a different, longer-lasting sound and it is a good idea to discuss this. They can play melody but it must be very slow music. More often they help the bass with the ostinato but there is some wonderful music in the Orff literature where the metallophones play a very haunting slow melody.

Examples of ostinatos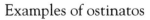

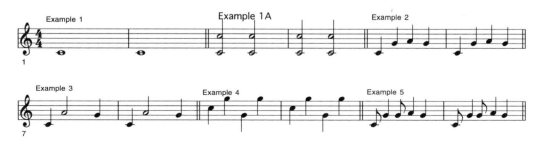

DAY 6 – SHORT COMPOSITIONS

A very short composition

Have the children work in small groups to create a short piece of music with an ostinato accompaniment.

These will be only eight or sixteen beats long so have them repeat them several times. Talk about the timbre of the different instruments. Discuss where the melody would best be played.

I find it useful to have the children work for 10 to 15 minutes and then show their work to the class. Some are certainly better than others and we can all learn from the good ones. Discussion of why certain things work well is a very large part of my classes on creativity.

Notes and Inspiration

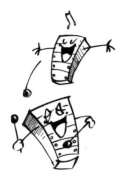

Improvisation 3
Creating Music to Words

Extension of language arts to musical form

This is an exercise for children who feel very comfortable with the instruments and the various sounds and effects they can make. I would recommend that some or all of the previous improvisation projects be tried before attempting this.

Give the children some poems

Here you must choose carefully, using poems where the scan will work with a fairly regular musical tune. The idea is to use the poem to create a melody.

Hint: Always give them several choices of poem. Always hand them written-out poems. Do not try to get them to memorize the poems.

These poems can scan in many ways. Say the poems to the children in several different manners, i.e. with the stress on different syllables.

Divide the children into small groups so they will not spend much time arguing. Ask them :

    1. To decide on a poem.

    2. To choose the meter or time signature that suits the spirit of the poem.

    3. To choose a mode or scale, to use for their poem.

(Advise the children to use C pentatonic, A pentatonic or one of the modes previously discussed. Within these scales it will be easier to create a good sound for the ostinato.)

4. Within the framework of these decisions, they should then try to create a melody that will fit the words.

Restrictions to be remembered from earlier improvisations

1. Question and answer

2. End on the tonic

3. Good melodies move mostly by step

At the end of day 1, I would definitely have a **time to share,** so that some of the groups who are feeling confused can benefit from some of the other groups. By the end of the second class you should have some good melodies.

DAY 3 AND DAY 4 – WRITING DOWN THE MUSIC

This next exercise, writing down the music they have created, is out of the Orff stream but nonetheless useful and interesting. This can take several classes. If the children cannot do this by themselves because of lack of experience with music notation, then do it on the board as **a class project.** This will involve choosing the best creations and then trying to write them down.

Melody first

Melody notes are usually easy. The children can often manage the note names very easily.

Rhythm next

This, you will find, is **much more difficult.**

You can start by getting the children to say the words in the rhythm they have chosen and then clap the strong beats for the music they have written. The bar line goes right before the beat with the clap and the beat with the clap is beat one.

Then they must notice and count how many times they clapped before a strong beat comes again – that is the number of beats in the bar. This is, of course, very simplified but it is a good way to begin.

The children will see the difference between 2/4 and 6/8 These often sound very similar with two basic beats to the bar. You can explain that 2/4 is made up of two parts of a rhythm like *apple* while 6/8 is made up of two parts of a rhythm like *merrily.*

Children often use a pickup in their compositions without realizing what they are doing rhythmically. This is another area for discussion.

Melody and rhythm together

Together you can work out the combination of the melody and the rhythm.

Once the melodies are written down, I print them, with the help of a computer so the children can see them printed out and other children can play them. Often the young composers will say, "That isn't what I wanted," and the process starts again. A tremendous amount of musical notation is learned from this exercise.

DAY 5 AND DAY 6 — CREATING AN OSTINATO

Adding the ostinato

Having written down the best melodies, you can now add other instruments to have an ensemble. I usually say one xylophone, one glockenspiel and one bass or metallophone per group, but you must choose according to the instruments you have available. If you have only a few, the whole class can work on this project. Ask for suggestions as to the best ostinato for a particular melody and try them out.

Emphasize that the rhythms of the ostinato must be simple so as not to compete with the melody. Also, the music will be more interesting if the ostinato is rhythmically very different from the melody. Ask them to use their ears to hear when the melody is clear or when it is being overtaken by some part of the accompaniment.

If they work on their own in small groups, quite a bit of help is required from the teacher.

DAY 7 AND DAY 8 — WRITING DOWN THE FINISHED MUSIC

Repeat the process of writing down the music, and again choose the best creations. This stage can be done either individually or as a class project.

I have done this each year for many years and am still amazed at the results. I have included a couple of their creations for you to try. While they are very simple, they are very effective and often defy the rules of music. I could not include the words around which they built their music as the poems were not their own. Nevertheless, they are interesting examples of children's classroom work.

You can see some examples of work done by children in my classes in a book edited by Lois Birkenshaw-Fleming titled *An Orff Mosaic from Canada/Orff au Canada: une mosaïque*. These include poetry around which the children created the music. In that case they were asked first to write poetry and then the best were selected for further musical composition. Definitely an integration of music and language arts. They had great fun writing the poems and seemed to be inspired by the fact that some would be chosen for further development into songs and eventually dramas.

DAY 9 AND DAY 10 — CREATE A DRAMA OR MOVEMENT SEQUENCE TO ACCOMPANY THE NEW COMPOSITION

Make the groups bigger and have some children act out the poems using the music that has been written. Some of the results will be amazing. I have often found that it is not the children who are technically proficient on the instruments who have wonderful little melodies in their heads. They gain great satisfaction from creating their own piece of music.

DAY 11 — ADDING PERCUSSION

Add percussion parts to pieces they have composed; for example, a steady drum beat can add a nice accent. The reason I leave this to last is that children can become very focused on the percussion instrument and forget to create the melody and the ostinatos. Still it adds a certain flavour to the finished composition and should be encouraged when the piece is near completion.

Examples of classroom work – Claude Watson School for the Arts, Grade 5, Spring 1996

Fishing is in C pentatonic scale.

Words for Fishing: The students who wrote "Fishing" created the music to one of the poems I had given them. However, when they came to dramatize their creation, they asked if they could write their own words:

 I went fishing, I reeled it in, It was a hundred pounder.
 I was so happy, so very happy, I jumped around in circles.

The scanning is not perfect but when they performed it they made it work.

The Pig is in C pentatonic scale.

Summer is in G Mixolydian mode.

Poetry and a Finished Presentation

This set of lessons shows how you can take a simple poem and turn it into a complete performance. Performance as an end result of learning the arts is very important. The arts are meant to be shared and therefore performed for an audience.

Included in this unit is the learning of a poem by a respected author, and the discussion of changing social issues.

Dramatizing a poem such as this with the children's own ideas is one type of approach for integrating language arts and Orff. The children can work at their own level. Some children will have very complicated ideas while other ideas will be very simple. They learn to put these together so the ideas work for every member of the group. This increases skills in group work, an absolute essential for the future workplace. This could also be very useful to students who are learning English as a second language. It helps them to play with words.

Children love to sing this particular song with its very simple accompaniment. This of course assumes that it is not the first piece ever played on the Orff instruments. It is not a particularly good beginning piece.

The children are also learning to be a good audience for their peers' productions.

They have probably enjoyed the experience of combining music and poetry and are ready for the next project.

Notes and Alterations

Poetry and Orff

Bed In Summer by R. L. Stevenson

In winter I get up at night,
And dress by yellow candle light.
In summer quite the other way,
I have to go to bed by day.

I have to go to bed and see
The birds still hopping on the tree,
Or hear the grown-up people's feet,
Still going past me in the street.

And does it not seem hard to you,
When all the sky is clear and blue,
And I should like so much to play,
To have to go to bed by day?

This is a wonderful poem, easy to learn and understand, which addresses an issue that is often important to children – "Why do I have to go to bed so early?"

DAY 1 – DISCUSS THE POEM

After reading the poem and talking about all the concepts – for example, candlelight for those who have never experienced living without electric power – the children can **dramatize the poem.** It is probably easiest to assign each group of three or four children one verse to work on. Children can come up with the most novel ways to express the words, ways that would never occur to an adult, so I think the most important first step is let them do it with no help from you and allow almost anything that is even close – sex and violence not permitted. I have seen rap tunes for the birds in the trees; I have seen a lumberjack get rid of those birds (from these supposedly ecologically aware children); I have seen summer lost because it went the other way.

DAY 2 – FURTHER DISCUSSION OF THE VARIOUS PARTS

(Optional) All of these ideas give you substance for further discussion if that is what you want to have. If you have no time for these extras then simply enjoy their interpretations.

Day 3 — sound effects to enhance the drama

I encourage them to **use an instrument to help their drama.** Each group is allowed only one instrument. (The reason for this is that the children concentrate entirely on the percussion instruments and forget the other purpose of the exercise. One instrument only improves the focus.) They must think of all the different sounds one instrument can make. This gives them time to continue work on their dramas while adding something new. The choice of instrument is theirs within certain parameters, but class discussion can arise around the best choices and how well they worked. Could other sounds be made on the chosen instruments? I never allow the use of the piano, partly because of the tuning, but you might feel differently about this.

Day 4 and Day 5 — learn the song

The music that is presented here is a very gentle piece of music expressing bedtime in the early 1900s. I would teach that only after I have worked on the drama so that the style of the music does not influence the drama presentations.

The song is easy to sing and the Orff parts are easy to perform. The bass is not absolutely necessary but a nice addition if you have the instrument. You will note that although the piece is in F major, I have written the Orff parts so as to avoid B♭ as I find it a nuisance changing all the B's to B♭'s. If you do not find this a problem, you might like to rewrite some of the accompaniment. You can see I left the B♭ for the bass as that is only one instrument to change.

BED in SUMMER

Words by Robert Louis Stevenson; Music Traditional arranged by Alice Brass

In   Win -ter I   get   up   at   night and   dress by yel- low   can - dle light. In   Sum - mer quite the
I   have   to   go   to   bed   to   see. The   birds still hop-ping   on   the tree. Or   hear   the grown up
And   does   it   not seem   hard to   you when   all   the sky   is   clear   and blue and   I   should like so

Glockenspiel

Xylophone   Metallophone

Bass

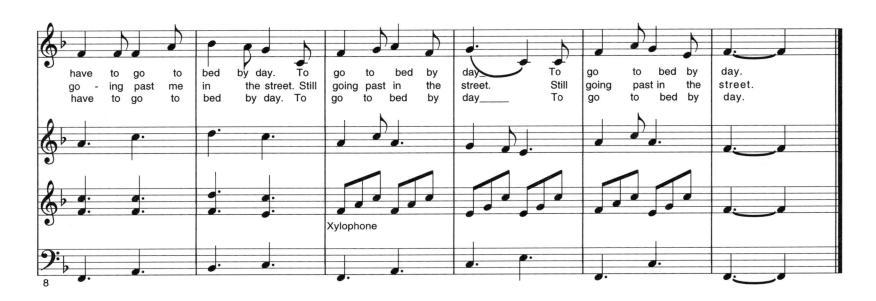

have   to   go   to   bed   by   day. To   go   to   bed   by   day_____   To   go   to   bed   by   day.
go -   ing   past me   in   the street. Still   going past in   the   street.   Still   going   past in   the   street.
have   to   go   to   bed   by   day. To   go   to   bed   by   day_____   To   go   to   bed   by   day.

Xylophone

Day 6 and Day 7 – recorder (optional)

Recorder practice

If you are teaching recorder, the melody is quite easy to play and provides some slow practice on F which is often a problem.

Days 8, 9 and 10 – assembling the work into a production

Prepare for chaos. Once the children have their dramas in some order and have learned the music, it is time to assemble the piece. I would ask for their input on this. One suggestion is the familiar rondo form with a verse of singing, a verse of drama, etc. Some children will do the dramas, some will play the Orff instruments, some can play the recorder, and all the children will sing. Don't expect it to work very well the first or second time you try, but as they get the ideas firm in their minds the presentation will improve.

At this point you can have quite a lot of input. At Claude Watson, I always have to work within a time restriction for the final production – 5 to 6 minutes is the normal limit. The chidren's creations are often much longer than this and we spend a lot of time discussing what can be cut without destroying their work. It is interesting to see how successful they can be at this exercise when they know that something must be cut if they want to perform. It is also interesting to see how fair they are to the work of their peers. They usually realize that the whole production benefits from the cuts.

This may be day 8, 9 and 10 and even more depending on your setup and the level of sophistication you are trying to achieve.

Day 11 – creating an introduction and an ending

Having developed the work this far, the children will realize they need a beginning and an ending, and again, turn this over to them. Do they want a dramatic ending or a quiet gentle ending? One group I saw did a sign-off commercial from the television to end it all. Another group of children finished off with "A hard knock life" because they were all in bed when they wanted to be outside.

This could also take several classes.

Day 12 – a final performance

Put it all together and if it merits an audience, try to find one – another class, another teacher, the principal, parents, whoever will make the best audience in this case. Most children love performing and their creations will improve when they know a performance is at the end of their work.

I do not encourage much in the way of costumes although the children love to create the odd prop. Coloured T-shirts and blue jeans, with shorts for summer or long pants for winter, make good uniform performance outfits. A hat or a scarf can often add just enough variety to increase the interest.

Closing

Have courage to experiment with some of these ideas.

Let the children's ingenuity and creativity lead you through these lessons. You must of course know ahead of time what you want but do not worry if the children take you in a completely different direction.

These are my ideas but I have written them down only to encourage you to explore with your children the structure and form of music. You should take these ideas and go your own way.

Children love Orff music and the Orff approach to learning. The pleasure they get from their final results is worth all the effort to get them there.

Appendices

GLOSSARY

CANON: A composition in which one part is imitated strictly in another part at any pitch or time interval. The imitation starts after the part to be imitated has been heard.

ECHO CLAPPING: The clapping, snapping, stamping, etc. of patterns performed first by the leader then by the group.

FOUND SOUNDS: Sounds made using everyday materials like door keys, paper, music stands, pencils on desks, etc.

HAIKU: Strictly defined, it is a Japanese lyric poem of a fixed 17-syllabic form that often simply points to a thing or pairing of things in nature that has moved the poet.

IMPROVISATION: The act of rendering music or body movement with little or no preparation.

MIRRORING: Actions in body movement or body percussion such as clapping, snapping, etc. where one person reflects exactly and simultaneously the movement of another.

OSTINATO: A repeated musical figure played as an accompaniment to a melody or song.

PATSCHEN: Patting the right hand on the right knee and the left hand on the left knee usually simultaneously.

PENTATONIC SCALE: A five-tone normally whole-tone scale which omits the fourth and seventh tones of the major scale. It can be built on the tonic of the major scale, and thus C pentatonic is CDE GA, or it can be built on the sub-mediant of the major scale and be A CDE G.

QUESTION AND ANSWER: The execution of a phrase of melody and/or rhythm which seems to ask a question by not ending on the tonic, followed by a similar answering phrase usually ending on the tonic or a strong beat.

RONDO: A musical form resulting from alternating the main theme or A section with other contrasting sections. The A section is repeated between each entry of another section. For example: ABACADA.

ROUND: A "circle canon", that is, a canon in which the melody is repeated at the same pitch level.

TIMBRE: Tone colour or the difference between tones of the same pitch produced by different instruments.

CURRICULUM GUIDELINES

It is often necessary to justify a program such as Orff in terms of a stated curriculum. The following is an outline of how a program following some of the ideas in this book could suit an individual curriculum. Educational curricula are often changing but the basic outline usually remains.

Often sections dealing with the arts are very specific and very encouraging, giving clear directions for the purpose of the arts and the need for children to be involved in the arts.

Colours of the Rainbow and *Fall* deal with expression of feeling through language, movement and music. It is desirable that students use a variety of forms to communicate information and describe feelings. Constructing and then acting out these poems gives children these communication experiences.

Several of the projects deal with the form of the music. *Canon in Music and Movement* explores the canon form while *A Rondo for Rhythm Instruments* explores a rondo. The improvisation lessons explore the form of question and answer as it relates to music.

Improvisation 1, 2, and 3 involve discussion of types of musical scales, the uses of rhythm and how it can change your music and the choice of melody for a vocal line. If you then try to notate the students' work with them, you cover many other theoretical sides of music – note values, clef signs, key signatures, time signatures to name a few.

As well, these improvisation projects experiment with techniques that are specific to each of the arts – dance, drama, music and visual art. At an older level improvisation can be used to express ideas and feelings.

The use of the different timbres of the Orff instruments created to accompany the melodies allows discussion of tone colours and how they work best together.

When the Orff instruments are used for accenting various aspects of a drama, tone colour is again being explored.

As a side effect we enter the world of science by discussing rainbows. The students should ask questions about the world around them and investigate phenomena in their environment. Other areas of the academic curriculum can be similarly explored.

The development of the ideas to a finished presentation follows the basic conventions to organize classroom performances and bigger presentations to parents and the general public.

In the particular poem I have chosen here, *Bed In Summer*, the children are comparing their experience with that of children in the days before electricity. They try to interpret what the author is saying and why it was appropriate in that time when perhaps it is not now. This shows how music can be used as a means of communication to discuss other ways of life.

There are no doubt many other ways that Orff activities meet the requirements of a curriculum. I have included these few to explain that while Orff may seem merely to be playing with the children, a lot of integrated music education is taking place in a very happy surrounding.

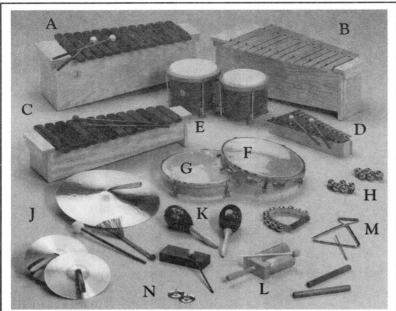

Courtesy Studio 49/ Waterloo Music

A SELECTION OF **O**RFF INSTRUMENTS

A – Alto Xylophone
B – Alto Metallophone
C – Soprano Xylophone
D – Alto Glockenspiel
E – Bongo Drums
F – Tambourine
G – Hand Drum

H – Bells
J – Cymbals
K – Maracas
L – Wood Blocks and Claves
M – Triangle
N – Finger Cymbals

Where to get more information

If you like the ideas in this book and would like to know more about Orff and the Orff approach to learning, you can attend Orff workshops, conferences and Orff courses. Many music publishers have displays at these conferences and workshops where you can purchase books and equipment to enhance your teaching. As well, this is often a place to make contacts and friends who will help you further with your program. To find out where and when these events are taking place you can contact the following organizations:

In Canada:
    Carl Orff Canada
    49 Kenora Street, Ottawa, ON K1Y 3K7
    Phone: 613-729-7129
    www.orffcanada.ca

In the U.S.A:
    The American Orff Schulwerk Association (AOSA)
    P.O. Box 391089, Cleveland, OH 44139-8089
    Phone: 216-543-5366. Fax: 216-543-2687
    www.aosa.org/contact/default.asp

Also by Alice Brass – *Orff Explorations*

In this sequel to *Orff Day by Day*, Alice Brass stresses improvisation and creativity with ten Orff projects, including several that incorporate poetry, visual arts and dances. Her clear step-by-step approach has helped many teachers bring the spirit of the Orff approach to their classroom activities. **ISBN 1-896941-34-6, $20.00**